Fitness and Fun for Children

Barbara Roberton

PSL

Patrick Stephens
Wellingborough, Northamptonshire

First published 1987

British Library Cataloguing in Publication Data

Roberton, Barbara
Fitness and fun for children.
1. Exercise for children — Physical
fitness for children
I. Title
613.7'042   RA781

ISBN 0-7225-1413-1

*Patrick Stephens Limited is part of the
Thorsons Publishing Group*

Printed and bound in Great Britain

My grateful thanks to all the children in
Fitness and Fun:

Tiny Tots — Emily Cox, Victoria Elmore,
Zara Turnbull

Older Children — my two daughters, Nicola
and Katy Rowe

Dedicated to children everywhere

Contents

Introduction

This book is for kids of all ages; from the very small to the nearly grown up. It doesn't matter how young you are or how old you are, you can have lots of fun with exercise. You can exercise on your own, or with your friends. You may even find Mummy and Daddy joining in, too.

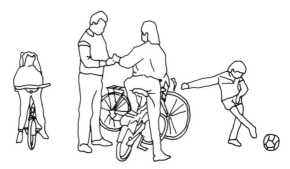

About Food

Feeling hungry is a sign that your body needs food. Some foods, like eggs, milk, cheese and fish, contain lots of protein. They help you grow and keep you fit and strong.

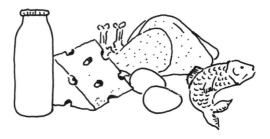

You also need food to give you energy. Foods which contain starch and sugar such as bread, potatoes, pasta and chocolate give you energy. You use up a lot of energy when you play games and exercise.

Butter, meat and fried foods contain fat. Fat keeps you warm, but it is not a good idea to eat too much fat. Healthy people eat a mixture of all kinds of food. We call this a balanced diet.

Your body also needs vitamins and minerals to keep healthy, Fresh fruit and vegetables contain vitamins and minerals.

Fat children make fat adults so do be careful what you eat. An apple or a carrot is much better for you than a bag of sweets, and is also good for your teeth.

About You

Take a good look at yourself in the mirror. Now give yourself a great big smile into that mirror — clean, white, healthy teeth — I hope. Look after your teeth, they have to last a long time.

Now then, how about the way you stand. Are you all saggy?
Stand up tall, tummy pulled in and your shoulders back. You will feel taller and lighter immediately, and it shows on your face too! Keep smiling, it will make you look good. When you look good you feel good!

About Sleep

Get plenty! You need sleep to replace all the energy you have used up throughout the day, and to make you feel well and ready to tackle the new day. If you don't get enough sleep you will find that you get irritable and miserable.

Now for the Exercises

Always remember IF IT HURTS — STOP! Never do anything that hurts you.

Tiny Tots

Take off your shoes and make sure you are wearing something comfortable like a tracksuit or a leotard. No hanging jewellery or buckles that might hurt you. Ask Mummy to put on your favourite record. Something really bouncy and jolly.

'Lets start at the very beginning — a very good place to be.
We start by counting 1, 2, 3. Jump up and down and follow me.'

(1)

Jumping up and down on the spot **(1)**.

(2)

(3)　　　　**(4)**

Jump up and down, swing your arms down by your side and really bend your knees **(2)**.

Run on the spot **(3)**.

Spring from foot to foot, sideways **(4)**.

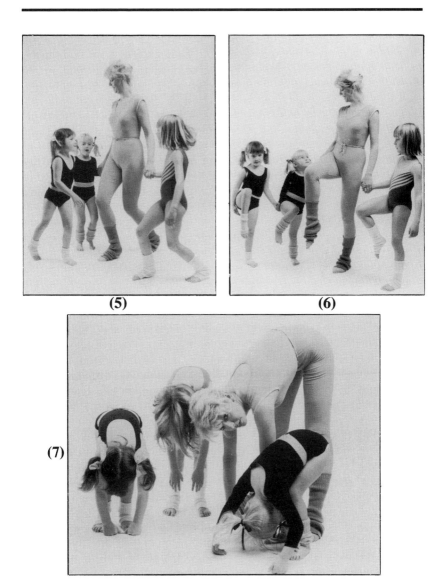

(5)

(6)

(7)

Now from front to back (5).

Skip on the spot lifting up your knees as high as you can for as long as you can (6).

Now have a flop and rest for a moment or two (7).

(8)

(9)

(10)

Gallop sideways — first in one direction and then in the other direction **(8)**. Be careful not to pull each other over if you are doing it with friends!

Skip around the room, swinging your arms and lifting up your knees as high as you can **(9)**.

Then flop and have a rest! **(10)**

(11)

(12)

Sit on the floor, on a mat or a blanket, legs out straight and make your toes wave — one foot, then the other and then both feet together **(11)**.

Try and reach your toes, without bending your knees **(12)**. Keep trying until you reach, but don't hurt yourself. Remember, IF IT HURTS — STOP.

(13)

(14)

Fold in half, put your head on your knees and touch your toes **(13)**. Then stretch up **(14)**. Try to do ten folds if you can.

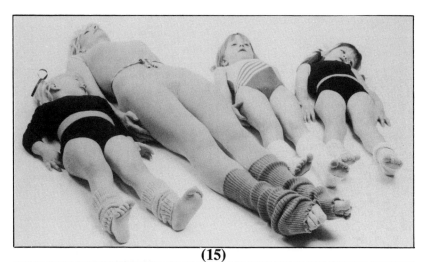

(15)

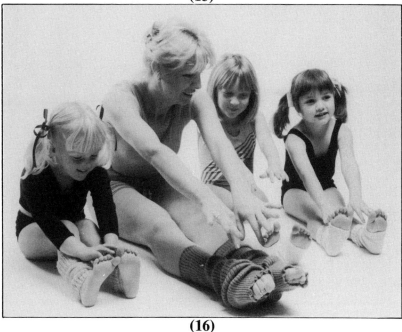

(16)

Lie down flat **(15)** and then sit up, keeping your feet down **(16)**. Say 'Hello' to your feet and lie back down again. See how many times you can do it. But don't hurt yourself.

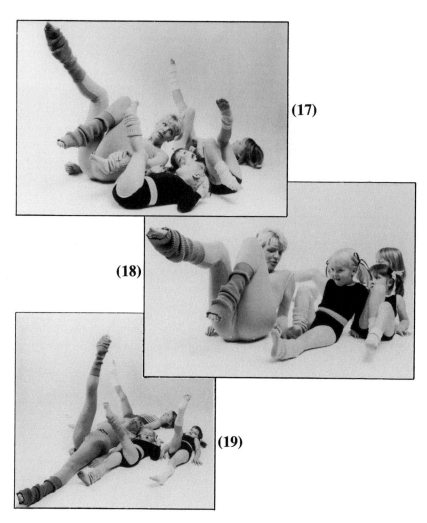

(17)

(18)

(19)

Lie down flat, put your hands under your bottom to protect your back, and cycle **(17)**. Make great big circles pointing your toes. Gradually make the circles smaller and faster until you are cycling as quickly as you can.

Sit up, lean back onto your elbows — and cycle **(18)**.

Straighten your legs and change legs in mid-air **(19)**.

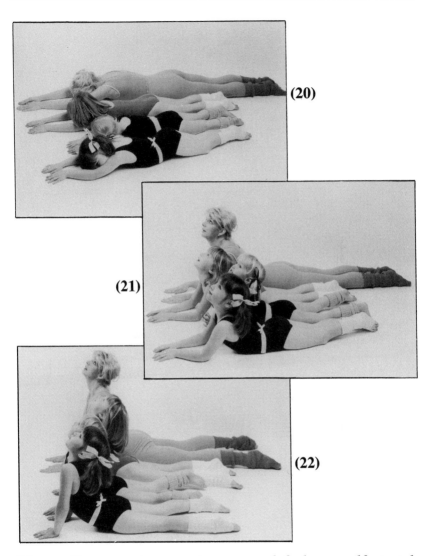

(20)

(21)

(22)

Now roll over onto your tummy and feel yourself stretch
from end to end **(20)**.

Very gently push yourself up with your hands **(21)**. Keep your
elbows tucked in and your shoulders down **(22)**. Carefully
bend from the waist. Don't push too hard.

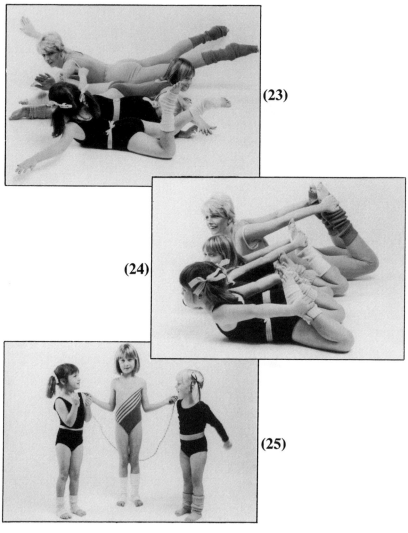

(23)

(24)

(25)

Make a star by lifting your arms and legs off the ground **(23)**.

Take hold of your ankles and gently pull **(24)**.

Now get up and skip — either with a skipping rope, (make sure it's safe) — or you can pretend to use a rope **(25)**.

(26)

(27)

Run on the spot for as long and as fast as you can (26). Have a flop and a rest (27). Then you can start all over again. Fun — isn't it?

For Older Children

There are lots of ways of exercising and having fun:

CYCLING

Cycling is wonderful exercise and it can be enjoyed by the whole family **(28)**.

SWIMMING

Everyone should learn to **swim**. Not only is it good exercise, but it opens up so many water sports for you to enjoy in safety **(29)**.

GAMES

Competitive **games** at school are a great way of keeping fit **(30)**.

JOGGING

Running or **jogging** can be enjoyed by the family **(31)**.

(28)

(29)

(30)

(31)

Fitness and Fun at Home

Don't sit in front of the television, get up, put on your favourite record and start to warm up. Make sure before you start that you are suitably dressed, no buckles or jewellery that might get caught up. It's not a good idea to exercise immediately after eating, you may feel sick or get cramp.

Warming up is very important and should be done for about five minutes. It gets the blood moving to all parts of your body at a quicker rate than normal and so ensures that you do not pull or strain the muscles you are working. Tights and leg warmers will keep your muscles warm and prevent them from cooling down too quickly, which will also help to prevent any injury.

Warm-up

Stand up tall, shoulders back, tummy pulled in and walk. Stretch your arms up above your head. Do this for a few minutes **(32)**.

Throw your legs up in front of you, as you continue round the room **(33)**.

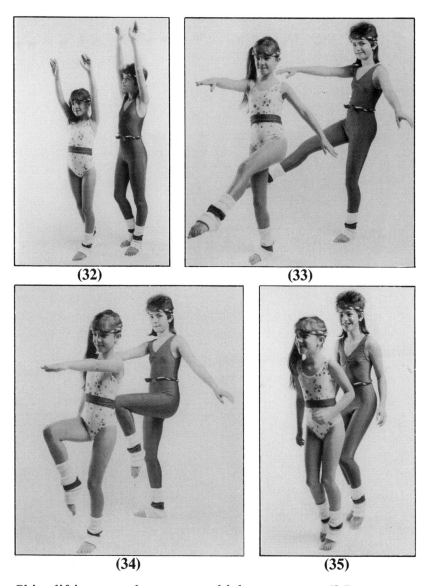

(32)   (33)

(34)   (35)

Skip, lifting your knees up as high as you can **(34)**.

Then jog around the room. Feel yourself getting really warm and loosened up ready for exercising **(35)**.

Toe Touching

Can you touch your toes? Start by touching the right toe with the left hand **(36)**. Then the left toe with the right hand **(37)**. Next take both hands down between your legs, touch the floor three times and then stretch up **(38)(39)**.

You may need to bend your knees a little to begin with. This soon won't be needed. Always use bouncy music, it makes it so much more fun.

(36)

(37)

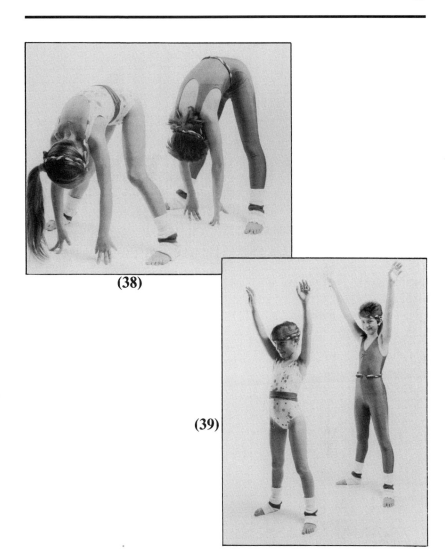

(38)

(39)

This will get rid of any stiffness in your legs and back. You will feel really loose.

You could also try taking both hands over to each foot.

Then, place your feet together and try touching your toes.

Leg Lifts

A lovely simple exercise to get your legs and thighs working. All you do is jump and lift your knee as high as you can. First one leg, then the other **(40)**. Swing your arms freely and enjoy it. Sing along to the music if you feel like it. Keep going for as long as you feel comfortable. If you breathe in through your nose and out through your mouth it will stop you panting.

Jump your feet apart and back together **(41)**. Do this four times with you arms by your side, then four times taking your arms up to form an 'X' **(42)**. Do this about ten times then have a wriggle and a rest.

(40)

(41)

(42)

Waist
Pushes

Do you struggle to get your tight jeans on? Well here is a super waist trimming exercise. Stand up straight, feet apart and push from the waist. Have your hand on your leg and try to reach your ankle. Push four times on each side and then eight times side to side. Do the whole thing ten times **(43)**.

Try the same exercise with your arm outstretched ten times **(44)**.

(43)

(44)

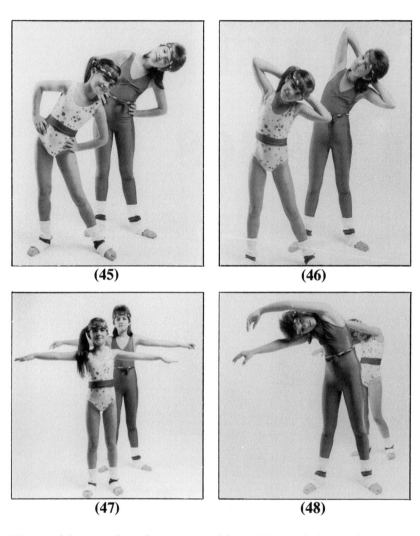

(45)

(46)

(47)

(48)

Then with your hands on your hips **(45)**, and then with your hands behind your head **(46)**.

Stand up straight, arms outstretched **(47)**. Take your right hand in an arc, over your head to touch your left hand **(48)**. Repeat twenty times on each side and you will soon be delighted how easily your jeans do up.

(49)

(50)

(51)

Now try some 'disco' pushes. Feet apart, one hand on your hip, and point with the other hand in all directions. Up in the air **(49)**, to the side **(50)**, to a diagonal and across your body **(51)**. Then repeat with the other arm.

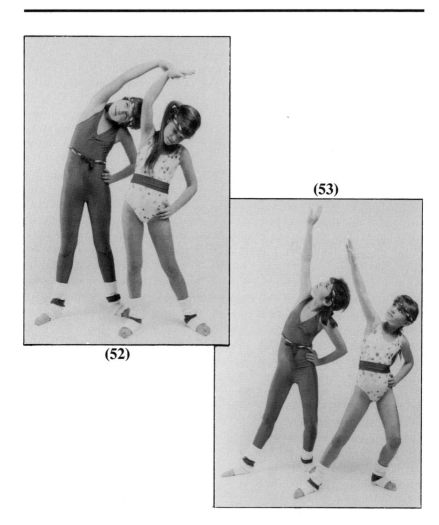

(53)

(52)

Stand with your feet apart and push from the waist, taking your arm over your head **(52)**. Push four times one way then four times the other way. Keep going as long as you can.

This time as you push, turn the palm of your hand to the ceiling and bend the leg which is supporting you **(53)**. Four pushes to each side at least ten times.

Floor Work

Let's lie down and do some floor work. These are great for flattening your tummy and toning your thighs and hips. It helps to have a mat or a thick towel. It cushions your back and it stops you sliding about.

Let everything go for a moment or two. Discover all your muscles, start by tightening your toes, then release them, work your way up through your body, calves, thighs, bottom, tummy, take a deep breath in through your nose hold for about four counts and then let everything go as you breathe out through your mouth **(54)**.

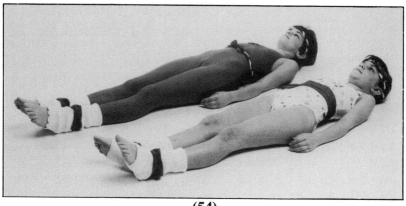

(54)

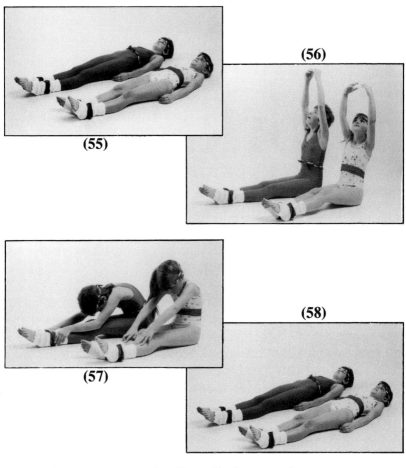

(55) (56) (57) (58)

Remember, never strain. Do all the exercises at your own pace and build up gradually. But don't be lazy!

Lie flat **(55)**, then sit up, stretching your arms above your head **(56)**. Feel your diaphragm lift and any extra inches disappear. Fold in half, trying to put your head on your knees **(57)**. Sit up and lie back down again **(58)**. When doing any form of sit-ups always come up and go down through a curved spine. By curving the spine you will ensure that you don't hurt your back.

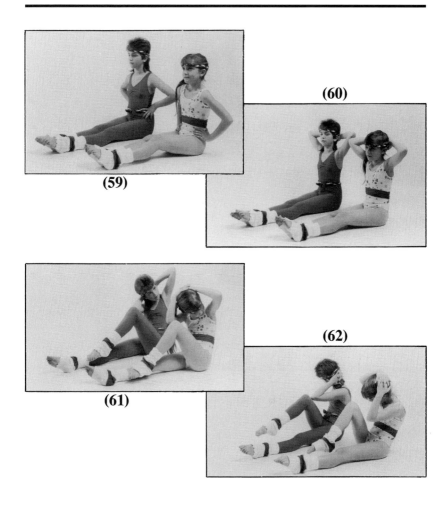

Next try sitting up with your hands on your hips **(59)**.

Place your hands behind your head and sit up **(60)**. You may find this difficult to begin with. Keep your tummy pulled in, you will soon be able to do it.

When you can do sit ups easily try placing your hands behind your head; as you sit up lift one knee up to touch the opposite elbow **(61)**. First one knee then the other **(62)**.

Cycling

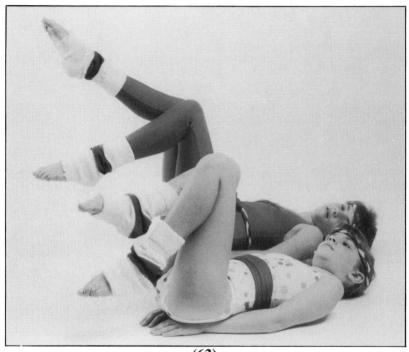

(63)

Lie flat and cycle for all you are worth **(63)**. Keep going for as long as you can.

Try cycling with your hands under your head **(64)**. This is much harder to do, but is really good for firming up your thighs.

Now change legs in mid air **(65)**, keeping them as straight as you can **(66)** and keep going for as long as you can.

(64)

(65)

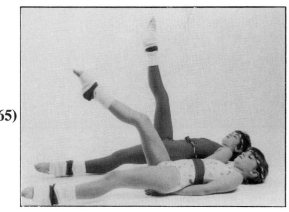

(66)

Hip Rolls

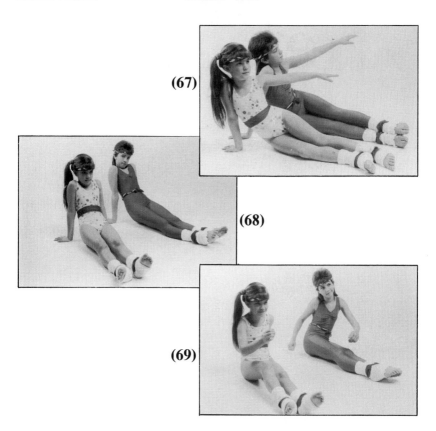

(67)

(68)

(69)

Roll away any extra inches and bounce away any bulges. Simply roll from side to side moving your weight about as you roll **(67)**.

Then bounce on your bottom **(68)**.

Walk on your bottom, forwards, then back again and then on the spot **(69)**. Sing whilst doing this. It's great fun.

Thigh Stretches

(70)

(71)

(72)

Sit up, feet apart and reach over to your left foot with your right hand **(70)**, then to your right foot with your left hand **(71)**. Now reach forward to both feet folding in half **(72)**, count three and sit up.

(73)

(74)

(75)

(76)

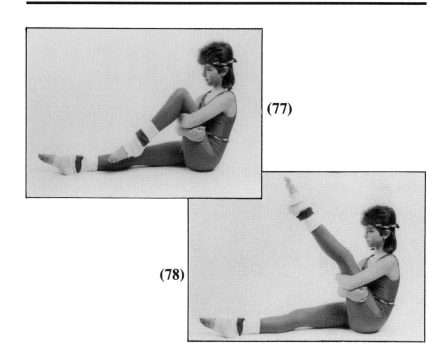

(77)

(78)

Reach over to your left foot with both hands and take hold of your foot, point your toes, then square your foot, point and square again then do the same thing to the other leg **(73)**.

Now fold in half and point and square both feet together **(74)**.

Bring your legs together, reach forward **(75)** and hold your feet, point and square the toes, keeping your head as close to your knees as you can **(76)**. Then release and have a good wriggle.

Sit up straight and take hold of your leg underneath the knee **(77)**. Gently extend the leg, pointing your toes **(78)**. Turn your ankle first in one direction, then in the other, then wave it up and down. Now the other leg.

For Your Back

(79)

(80)

(81)

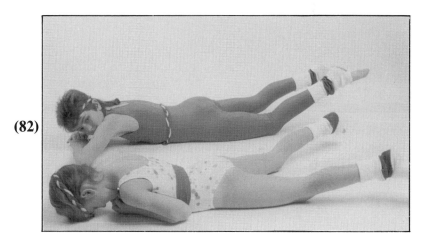

(82)

Roll over onto your tummy, push up from the waist with the help of your hands **(79)**. Make sure you keep your elbows in and your shoulders down. Push gently, don't strain **(80)**. Now stretch your hands out in front of you and lift your arms and legs together — like superman! **(81)** *Use slower music for these exercises.*

Legs apart, lift them off the ground, bring feet together, open and let them down **(82)**. Do five of these leg lifts.

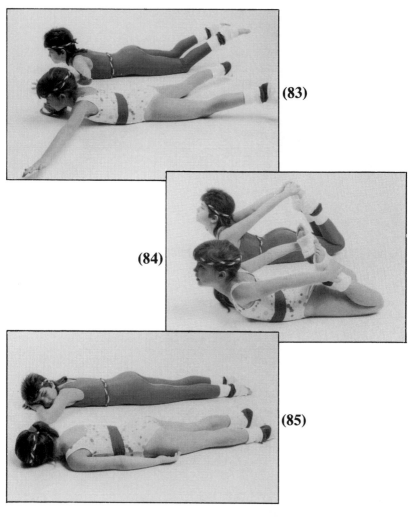

(83)

(84)

(85)

Now lift your legs and arms together so that you make a star **(83)**.

Take hold of your ankles and gently pull up **(84)**. IF IT HURTS — STOP!

Flop and have a rest for a few seconds **(85)**.

Thigh Toners

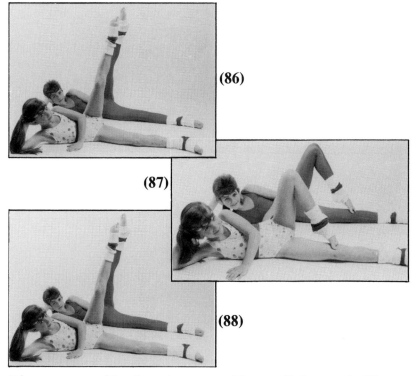

(86)

(87)

(88)

Lie on your side, keeping your hips well forward. Throw your leg up sideways. Keep going for as long as you can **(86)**.

Then flex your leg from your knee **(87)(88)**. Repeat on the other leg.

(89)

(90)

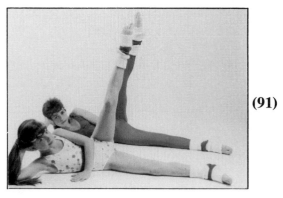

(91)

Still lying on your side, bend in your knee **(89)**, stretch it forward **(90)**, lift it up and put it back to the starting position **(91)**. Try about six on each side.

Jump Up!

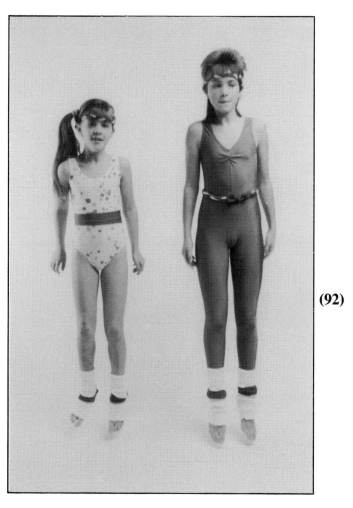

(92)

Jump up! Bounce on the spot, shaking your arms and hands
(92).

(93)

(94)

(95)

Pull up onto your toes **(93)**, and bend right down into a crouch position **(94)**. Keep going up and down for as long as is comfortable **(95)**.

Sway from side to side, bending at the waist. Do about ten sways, then sweep round in a circle, letting your hands touch the floor as you go round **(96)(97)(98)**.

Now sweep round and bend your knees on the downward sweep. First in one direction and then in the other **(99)(100)**.

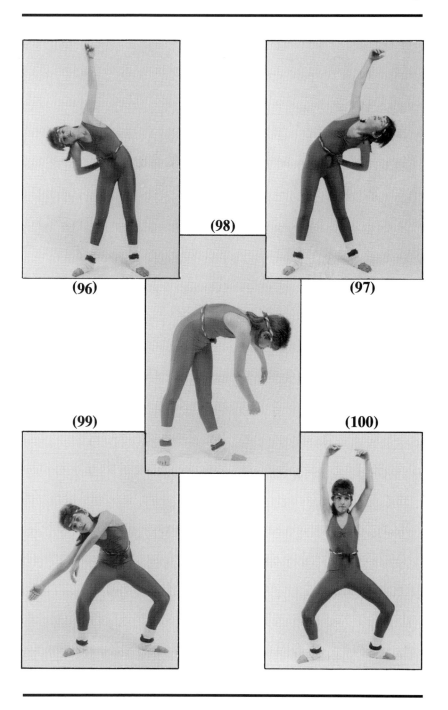

(96)

(97)

(98)

(99)

(100)

Leg Stretches

(101)

(102)

Stand up straight, arms stretched out to the side **(101)**, take a big step forward **(102)**, and then step feet back together. Let your supporting leg bend. Try ten on each leg.

(103)

(104)

(105)

Step forward, supporting leg bent **(103)**, and push over your knee, put your hands on the ground **(104)**. Transfer your weight from the front foot onto both feet, at the same time straightening the leg **(105)**. Try six on each leg.

(106)   (107)

(108)

Stand up straight, step back with your right leg **(106)** and then kick it through as high as you can **(107)** — GOAL! Keep kicking through with the right leg until the supporting leg tells you to stop. Then do the same with the left leg.

Now stand up straight, stretch your left arm out at shoulder height, using your right leg, kick your hand **(108)**. Ten with the right leg, then change arms and kick your hand with the other leg.

Hula Hips!

(109)

(110)

Stand up straight, hands on your hips and roll your hips round. Clockwise and then anticlockwise. Really wriggle those hips! **(109)**

If you have a hula hoop, now is the time to get out and use it. You can almost see the inches fall off as you hula that hoop! **(110)**

Waist Turns

(111)

(112)

(113)

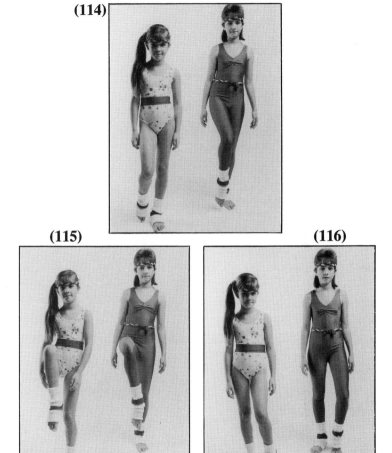

(114)

(115)

(116)

Stand up tall, feet apart, arms at shoulder height at 90°. Keeping your hips and knees perfectly still, turn from the waist, at least twenty times **(111)(112)(113)**.

Then try a double push to each side.

Run on the spot **(114)**, gradually lift your knees higher and higher **(115)**. Then work your way down, lower and lower until you are pushing from one foot to the other **(116)**.

Cool Down

(117)

(118)

(119)

Cooling down is as important as warming up. It is a slowing down of the body. The muscles need to cool down and slow down gradually in order to prevent strains and pulls.

Skip around the room **(117)**.

Then trot for a few minutes and slow right down to a walk, keeping your tummy pulled in and your shoulders back **(118)**.

Feel everything relax in your body and finally flop! **(119)**

Relaxation

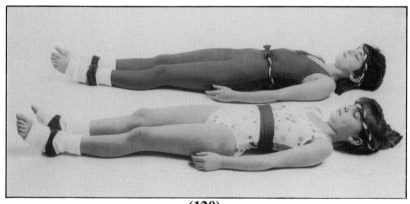

(120)

Choose a slow peaceful piece of music. Put on a warm sweater and lie down **(120)**.

Close your eyes and let every muscle in your body flop.

Let yourself float away for a few minutes.

When the music stops, have a wriggle and sit up when you are ready.

You will feel wonderfully relaxed and rested. Your heart and pulse will be beating normally. You are ready for anything.

HAVE FUN!

Fitness and Fun Chart

Start at number one and work your way up to fitness

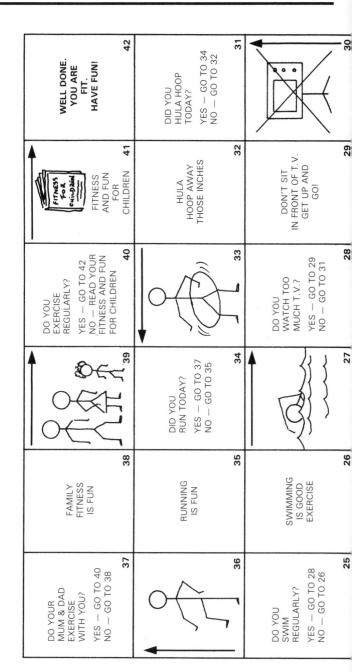

DO YOUR MUM & DAD EXERCISE WITH YOU? YES — GO TO 40 NO — GO TO 38 **37**	FAMILY FITNESS IS FUN **38**	*(figures)* **39**	DO YOU EXERCISE REGULARLY? YES — GO TO 42 NO — READ YOUR FITNESS AND FUN FOR CHILDREN **40**	FITNESS AND FUN FOR CHILDREN **41**	WELL DONE. YOU ARE FIT. HAVE FUN! **42**
(figure) **36**	RUNNING IS FUN **35**	DID YOU RUN TODAY? YES — GO TO 37 NO — GO TO 35 **34**	*(figure)* **33**	HULA HOOP AWAY THOSE INCHES **32**	DID YOU HULA HOOP TODAY? YES — GO TO 34 NO — GO TO 32 **31**
DO YOU SWIM REGULARLY? YES — GO TO 28 NO — GO TO 26 **25**	SWIMMING IS GOOD EXERCISE **26**	*(figure)* **27**	DO YOU WATCH TOO MUCH T.V.? YES — GO TO 29 NO — GO TO 31 **28**	DON'T SIT IN FRONT OF T.V. GET UP AND GO! **29**	*(figure)* **30**

19 ARE YOUR JEANS TOO TIGHT?
YES – GO TO 20
NO – GO TO 22

18

7 DID YOU SMILE THIS MORNING?
YES – GO TO 10
NO – GO TO 8

6

20 WAIST PUSHES WILL HELP

17 TOE TOUCHING LOOSENS YOUR LEGS

8 SMILE AND THE WORLD WILL SMILE BACK AT YOU

5 BREAKFAST IS ESSENTIAL TO START THE DAY

21

16 DID YOU TOUCH YOUR TOES TODAY?
YES – GO TO 19
NO – GO TO 17

9

4 DID YOU EAT BREAKFAST?
YES – GO TO 7
NO – GO TO 5

22 DID YOU EAT CHIPS AT LUNCHTIME?
YES – GO TO 23
NO – GO TO 25

15

10 DID YOU CYCLE TO SCHOOL?
YES – GO TO 13
NO – GO TO 11

3

23 TOO MUCH FAT IS BAD FOR YOU

14 AN APPLE IS BETTER FOR YOU AND YOUR TEETH

11 CYCLING IS A GOOD FORM OF EXERCISE BUT BE CAREFUL

2 SLEEP REPLACES YOUR ENERGY AND STOPS YOU FROM BEING IRRITABLE

24

13 DID YOU HAVE AN APPLE RATHER THAN SWEETS AT PLAYTIME?
YES – GO TO 16
NO – GO TO 14

12

1 DID YOU GET AT LEAST 8HRS SLEEP LAST NIGHT?
YES – GO TO 4
NO – GO TO 2

Fitness and Fun Alphabet

A A is for alive — your greatest gift. Make the most of it and treat your body with the respect it deserves.

A is also for apple and appetite, so if you feel hungry between meals have an apple. It won't ruin your appetite and will help you stop getting acne.

B B is for beauty. Beauty comes from within, so take care of your body and your natural beauty will show.

B is also for bathing — regular bathing makes you nice to know.

C C is for cycling — good exercise for all the family.

C is also for common sense, cosmetics and clothes. Instead of spending lots of money on clothes and make-up spend some time working your body and having confidence in the real you.

D D is for diet. Fat children make fat adults, so do be careful what you eat.

D is also for dentist — your smile is your greatest asset. Visit your dentist regularly.

E

E is for exercise. You owe it to your body to exercise regularly.

E is also for eyes — make them sparkle. Don't watch too much television.

F

F is for Fitness and Fun for Children. Use it every day.

F is also for fibre, fruit and fish — all essential for a healthy diet.

G

G is for get up and go. Get into the habit of exercising, make it part of your routine.

G is also for gently does it — always build up gently. IF IT HURTS — STOP.

H

H is health and happiness which go together hand in hand.

H is also for hair — keep it clean and healthy.

I

I is for your insides. Eat a healthy diet and it will show on the outside.

I is also for individual — you're your own best advert, so be proud of being an individual.

J

J is for jogging. Jogging on the spot is a great way of warming up.

J is also for jumping for joy — be glad to be alive.

K K is for keeping fit. A fit person is a happy person.

K is also for kidneys — keep yours healthy by drinking plenty of water.

L L is for life. Make the most of yours.

L is also for leotard and leg warmers — worn when exercising.

M M is for muscle toning exercises. Do yours often.

M is also for make-up — it's not how much you use, it's the way you use it!

N N is for natural. Use your body's natural rhythm and enjoy exercising.

N is also for nails — don't bite them.

O O is for overeating. Don't do it, eat sensibly and you won't get overweight.

O is also for opening your eyes — don't pretend you are not overweight when you know that you are.

P P is for posture. Stand up straight and have pride in the way you look.

P is also for pain. IF IT HURTS — STOP.

Q Q is for questions. Ask 'How can I improve myself?' Then do something about it.

Q is for quiet — allow yourself a few quiet moments to relax each day.

R

R is for relaxation. Learn to relax and not let petty irritations affect your life.

R is also for routine — make exercise and relaxation part of your daily routine.

S

S is for shape. You don't have to be skinny to have a good shape. Make the most of your good points and do something about the not so good ones.

S is also for smile — smile and the world smiles with you!

T

T is for toning. Exercise will tone the muscles in your tummy and your thighs.

T is also for time — make time to exercise.

U

U is for unwanted inches. Start now, eat sensibly and exercise regularly.

U is also for unique — each person is unique, so be yourself and have pride in your appearance.

V

V is for vitality. Exercise will increase your vitality and self-confidence.

V is also for voice — don't set other people's nerves jangling. Speak in a quiet, pleasant voice.

W W is for walk tall. You will be amazed at the difference it makes.

W is also for weight — eat sensibly and you won't need to watch yours.

X X is for extra. The extra fun you will get from exercising.

X is also for excess — all things in moderation.

Y Y is for You. Be your own best friend, look after your body.

 Y is also for yoga — a gentle way of exercise and relaxation.

Z   Z is for zest. The zest for life and for living it to the full.

 Z is also for 'zzzzzzzzz' — get plenty of sleep.